A Field Guide to Grief

If you've lost your partner to suicide

Kate Johnson

ISBN-13: 978-1511433440
ISBN-10: 1511433442

Library of Congress Control Number: 2015905385

CreateSpace Independent Publishing Platform
North Charleston, SC

Dedicated to All of Us

There is no law of conservation of grief
or conservation of loss.

Alas, my grief does not lessen yours,
as yours cannot not lessen mine.

I consciously honor all of us:

> Here's to the people we were before;
> and here's to the people we are after;
> And here's to the raw tender hope that
> pushes up in spite of all we've known
> and all we've lost.

Introduction

Once upon a time, I was married to a wonderful, charismatic, brilliant, tormented man. When we married, I had no idea that he was already losing a battle to the slow ravages of untreated depression. In the summer of 2003, I lost him to suicide.

The grief associated with suicide is complex, and resources are hard to find. This book is based on the content of a blog I wrote as a resource for people like me.

To anyone out there new to this or old to this, you know: There is nothing simple about this kind of loss. My story is not necessarily anyone else's. My reactions, my emotions, my thoughts, are all my own. But it makes sense to me to put this story out there, in hopes that it will help someone else feel less alone, less desperate, less desolate. And also, perhaps, provide a glimmer of hope if only by showing that even though something awful has happened and can never un-happen, years can pass, and that life—a good life—can happen too.

Please

Losing someone you love can be shattering. If you feel suicidal, get help. Please.

Call 911, or call a friend, or the national suicide hot line: 1-800-273-8255—those folks are excellent and amazing.

Or go to the emergency room. Tell them you need help.

Please, give yourself and those you love a little more time. Reach out. Ask for help.

Think about what you would want for a loved one, a dear friend, and treat yourself that way. Treat yourself as if you matter.

Because you do. You do. You do.

Contents

A Field Guide to Grief

If you've lost your partner to suicide

Right Away

You may feel as if you are drowning. As if you may die. As if somehow nothing will ever be ok again. That this is impossible. Unimaginable. And you would do anything anything anything to make this not have happened, and to make the feelings stop.

There can be crying or madness or feelings of near insanity. You may want to pound on the table or scream or collapse. You may find yourself falling backwards into quiet.

There is no right way.
Whatever is, is.

There can be dizziness and disorientation. There can be noises you cannot believe you are making. There can be a million hands on you, arms around you, but you are the kind of alone that feels so intense that you are not sure you will ever come back.

Somehow you get home or to a safe place. Somehow you hear people offering sympathies and astonishment for something you do not and cannot believe has happened. Somehow your body starts to shut down against auxiliary sources of input. You go deeper inside. There is the beginning of numb. There is an odd quiet.

Soon there will be questions from people in authority. You will talk with the police. Possibly the hospital. The medical examiner. You have conversations that feel impossible too. What is this life that you are living where you need to talk to these people? But you may. And you do. And they will ask hard questions. And you may or may not know the answers. Just be truthful.

If you are worried that you are numb and that somehow this means something bad about you, it doesn't. This feeling of numb, as you will see, is a gift. It is your Self protecting itself from the intensity.

See if you can allow yourself into the strange and foreign comfort that shock unwittingly provides. Do not feel as if you are not doing this right. There is no right. There is just doing this, surviving this. And you are: You are already doing this, one breath at a time.

Taking Care

Make sure someone calls your work and lets them know.

Make sure someone calls your family.

If you have children or pets, make sure they are cared for. Maybe this seems obvious, but in these first moments and days, you are in survival mode. And sometimes things, even really important things, get forgotten.

Night

Make sure you are safe. Make sure you do not get rid of your own lifelines by isolating yourself. Consider staying in one room while a friend or family member stays nearby—even if in a different room, or on the sofa...

You may sleep or you may not.

You may spend time remembering or you may not.

You may find your mind circling around and around and around, imagining what happened, why, and what it might have been like for your loved one.

You may find that you are swamped with regret—that you remember the last things you said and wish you had said something else, wish you had done something else.

You may find yourself crying so hard you are afraid you may never stop. Or you may lie there with a lump in your throat the size of Texas. Or you may be numb. Or any of a million things.

But if you find that you are feeling at all suicidal, please call for help, do not hesitate, do not worry about being a bother or not wanting to worry people—just get help. Call 911. Call a suicide hot line. Call even if you are just starting to think that somehow ending it, putting an end to the pain is the only thing that makes sense.

In this moment, making the pain stop may feel like the most important thing—but decisions you make right now may not be truly in your best interest, or in the interest of those you need to care for.

Hold yourself gently. Know you are doing the best you can. If you find yourself focusing on self-damaging thoughts, use the word Stop. Say it out loud if you need to. Each time you return to a painful thought, say Stop. Distract yourself any way you safely can. Bring yourself away from the troubling thoughts each time, gently and with self compassion.

Allowing yourself to sleep does not mean you are not grieving, or sad, or scared, or aware of how horrible things are.

Sleep is a place of deep and profound healing. Let yourself sleep if you can.

Helpers

There may be people around you trying to help.

Tell them what you need if you have the faintest idea what that is—if you need them to make calls for you, ask them. If you need space and silence, say so. If you need to have someone walk your dog, or just sit with you, say so.

Everyone feels powerless in this situation.
Everyone.
The helpers, the people who love you, they feel powerless too.

But it is not your job to take care of folks who are trying to take care of you. If you do not know what you need or want, you are totally allowed to say so.

Eating

You may not be eating what you should. Or you may be eating more than you did before, trying to fill up the hole that sits raw edged and throbbing in the center of your chest.

Or

you may not be eating at all.

Eat anyway.

Eat even if you cannot imagine eating.

Eat something that matters — something with calories.

If you cannot swallow past the lump, try ice cream, applesauce, a milkshake, a smoothie, a yogurt, instant breakfast...

You are in the midst of an emotional marathon, you need food, you need water. Think of it as fuel for survival.

Waking

You may wake up in the middle of the night or in the morning or in the afternoon. There may be a lull, a moment, a quiet peacefulness. And then there is the crushing feeling as you remember. When you realize it was not a dream. When you realize that you have lost so many precious things, including the ability to go back and un-do whatever you feel you have done that led to this moment.

If it is night, you may lie there and systematically torture yourself with thoughts of what might have been, if only… you may play the death in your head as you imagine it. You may play the finding, the losing, the horrible first moments over and over and over.

Tell yourself to Stop. If you can't stop, get up.

If you wake up and it is morning, there may be things you have to do. Difficult and crazy decisions you have to make. Where the body needs to go. What to do. You may have to talk with the police again. You may have to talk with the medical examiner again. You may talk with the funeral home. Cremation? Burial? Obituary?

Some of these choices you will need to make quickly. Others can wait.

Unbelievable as it seems, you can and will make these choices.

Things will cost more than you can imagine. Order more death certificates than you think you will need. You will need them for everything.

The funeral director is someone who may be able to help in more than one way—they may be able to offer insight and solace as someone who has been with death, including suicides, before.

Very few of us have.
None of us should have to.

To me, they offered this: This choice was not about me. It was not about love or the failure of love to perform miracles. Suicide is about the person who has killed themselves. This was their life. Suicide was their decision. They made the choice to die and to die this way.

Self Protection

Be self protective.

You do not owe anyone information or an explanation or details or anything else that you don't want to share. It is really easy to tell people too much, especially in the beginning, to share too much as you navigate through those amazingly difficult first days...

People will ask you things that you cannot believe they will ask:

How she/he did it, did you find them, did they leave a note, did you knew they were going to do it...

Come up with a simple line or two that conveys a non-negotiable boundary. Memorize it. Use it to give yourself time to decide what you want to share and what you don't and with whom.

"I am sure you'll understand that this is just too

painful for me to talk about".

Irrefutable.
Self protective.

Find a message that works for you and use it.

Crying

Your numbness might come and go. Tears may push through when you are driving or when you wake in the middle of the night or when you go to the bathroom at work. You may cry so hard that tears and snot and spit just spill from your face onto the ground and there is nothing you can do to stop it until it is good and done and over.

You may not be able to be with other people without them bringing it up, or perhaps more awkwardly, pointedly not bringing it up. You may not know what to say, or know if it is ok to laugh. Or what happens if you start to cry?

About crying: If you breathe out, a forceful breath blown through your mouth like you are trying to blow out a candle…and at the same time if you look up as far as you can with your eyes without moving your head and blink a lot, you can sometimes push through the immediate need to cry. Sometimes. Tell yourself you will let yourself cry as soon as you can. But the blowing, and the looking up and blinking can save you, even if it only brings you the 30 seconds you need to turn away, or close the door, or pull off the road.

Crying comes and goes. Times it will flood in and pin you down. Other times, days will pass with no tears at all. As times goes on, this pattern will repeat—times of big grief, and times of relative calm. Know that each will pass. The horrible sadness. The relative calm.

Music

Music is powerful.
It can be healing and comforting.

But

you may want to avoid listening to music that you
love, as you may forever associate it with this time.

Reminders

Things will remind you of him or her. Things you may not expect.

Sometimes, so innocently, you'll catch yourself thinking there is something you want to tell them, or something you'll show them next time you drive by... and then you'll realize, re-realize your loss, and you need to be gentle with yourself with what happens next. It may be laughter, or crying, or fury, or disbelief as you rediscover your circumstances. You may feel like an idiot for forgetting—how can you possibly forget? But remember, while yes, this has happened to you, *it is not who you are*. It is one giant sharp-edged piece of your experience. However big, however impossible to imagine, it is not everything and cannot be everything and will not be everything.

In any given moment, the thing that you are doing is surviving. That is what most humans do. We survive. We drive our cars carefully. We go to work. We eat. We sleep.

We dream. We see a hawk overhead and think of the person we have lost, tell ourselves we will tell them when we get home. And then we realize that it is not going to happen like that.

Marking Time

You may find you mark the time, most literally, looking at the clock each day thinking "now, now is when", and your heart will be broken with the thought.

And then, it will be days—one day since, two days since, three days since...

and then it will be a week,

and then, somehow, time passes, and it will be a month...

Identity

You may not even recognize yourself these days.

Sometimes you may feel as if you do not know what to do with yourself. or you do your days the old way, the way from before.

You go to work, come home, eat... but you are no longer the you that you were. People who don't know, treat you like you are normal. No one stops and stares at the grocery. But you are going through your days like a paper bag filled with broken glass.

You will find that some of the pieces of your old self are in that bag-- that some of the things that mattered still matter. But there are a lot of unfamiliar pieces too. Maybe some days you will look in the mirror and wonder who you are. You are no longer the person you were, you are no longer the person this had not happened to...

You wake up each day

day after day
this is the first thing you think about.

You may not even remember when you were worried about other things, your job maybe, or getting enough exercise. Now much of life may seem to be on automatic pilot—you get up, brush your teeth, go to work, interact as if you are normal, come home, eat, sleep.

But this loss, this pain is always with you. Sometimes you cannot believe there is not a gaping hole in your chest.

There is such loneliness in this. No one else is you. It is not as if someone else grieving with you would make you feel less alone. Of course, lots of other people are grieving too. It is just that no one can lessen the load of it for anyone else.

At night, when you close your eyes, it's just you.

Try to be gentle with yourself. A few months in, when the funeral is well over and people have returned to their lives, you will find yourself alone in a different way. You may need to seek out friends, they may no longer be seeking you out.

Sometimes just being around people, but not needing to interact—going to a bookstore, a coffee shop, the grocery store—can help you begin to reconnect to the broader circle of humanity in a way that is safe.

One of the most haunting things is feeling you no longer know yourself. And you may find yourself grieving, missing the person you had been.

There are nested losses. This is nested grieving. You are grieving the loss of your loved one, your friend, your partner, and also the loss of the you that you were.

Be compassionate with this person you are getting to know, this post-loss you. You may find that some parts of you want to be expressed now in new ways. you may find that you want to be creative, make music, paint, write. Do it. Explore what you are drawn toward. Sometimes traumas can kick us out of a rut of self-perception, and make us realize that there is more to us than we thought.

Support

There are support groups for survivors.
There are online resources.
There are therapists and clergy members.
There are healers for your body, heart and mind.

Seek out the help and support you need. There is trauma inherent in your loss.

If you find you are perseverating, repeating the same loops of memories or images over and over and over, there is help for that. EMDR and EFT are two techniques that you can learn and use to help yourself out of the spirals and seemingly endless loops.

You do not need to suffer, alone or otherwise.

And no, you don't deserve to suffer either.
Treat yourself with love and with compassion.

One Morning

There will be a morning when you wake up and you do not think of this first.

You will be astonished.

And then, you may feel a tidal-wave of guilt.

It does not mean you do not care, that you are not grieving, that you are not honoring the person you lost.

It does not feel as if this is true, but it is.

Holding Memory

You may feel that it is up to you to hold onto the rawness, the acute memories of the pain of the first days… as if somehow this holding of memories is keeping your loved one's existence alive, even though they are no longer here.

You may feel responsible to stay mired in grief, that your grief, the intensity of your ongoing grief is somehow is a testament to your love, to your loss.

You may feel it is up to you to keep thinking about them so they are not forgotten.

Feeling as if you, alone, are holding the memories of your loved one is a lot of weight to carry. See if you can find a way to lessen the feeling of responsibility.

Notice that there is a webwork of friends and family, of people who also knew them, and each one of you holds pieces of memory, not just you alone.

If you want to capture specific stories, do. You can write them down, record them, or tell them to someone.

It is not your responsibility to forever hold and guard evidence of their life.

Grief

Sometimes, just when you think you finally are getting it together, a new wave of unresolved grief surfaces, bubbles up or floods in.

Out of nowhere comes grief— grief for your loved one, grief for your past choices and feelings of powerlessness and, oh, the immensity of a thousand regrets… and what can you do in the midst of it as it swirls around and tries to suck you under?

Be kind to yourself.

You have made it through this cycle before. It will come and, then, however impossible it may feel right now
it will go.

Guilt

Guilt is one of the most insidious and persistent reactions to losing a loved one to suicide.

A million questions cycle back around and around and around. You may ask yourself if there was anything you could have done, if there was anything else you could possibly have done to prevent it...

You may retrace and replay conversations and decisions, interventions or choices.

Maybe you said you were going to leave.
Maybe you left.
Maybe you feel responsible.
Maybe they said you were.

But this was their choice.
Theirs.

Survivors Guilt

And then there is "survivors guilt".

What right do I have to a happy life?
What right do I have go on living?
What right do I have to love again?
To heal?
To be whole?

Choose to live your life. Choose to. Choose to over and over and over.

There is enough space in each of us for both the pain of unimaginable loss and the tender experience of living.

Trust

You may no longer trust yourself.

You may not trust your judgement or your ability to take care of yourself.

You may not trust yourself to choose people who are good for you, or trust your choices, or your ability to be self protective.

You may no longer trust your instincts or intuition.

Learning to trust yourself again, once that trust gets shaken, takes practice and awareness, but it mostly takes a kind of faith.

You did not knowingly create the situation or relationship that ended in this loss. You did not deliberately hurt yourself this way. This is not a ride anyone would sign on for if they knew.

Practice paying attention to your instincts, practice trusting yourself. As you meet new people, be aware of how your body feels. Warm and open? Or closed and careful. Navigate by feel.

You are wiser and able to be more self protective than you may believe right now.

Love

Love may find you.
New love.
An old love.
The desire to love.
The longing for love.

This is not infidelity.

This is life asserting itself in a desire to connect.

Trust yourself. Go as slowly as the most scared, the most wounded parts of you want to go.

Loving will not cause the feelings of loss to go away, or even lessen the grief.

Loving will help with loneliness, but not for the person that you were. Or the person you lost.

Or perhaps you feel like you want to be alone forever.

That you'll never trust anyone else again. That loving feels too dangerous. The threat of loss too large. Trust yourself with this too. For you, right now, it may be just not time. It may never be time.

Only you will know.

Judgement

Oh, people.

People may say the most horrible things. They may judge you if you are happy. They may judge you if you are too sad for too long. They may judge you if you date or fall in love. If you move. If you stay. If you're alone. They may judge you for holding on. They may judge you for letting go, or "moving on" (as if that is ever truly possible). They may judge you for eating too much, or eating too little, or being too "OK", or being too distracted, or working too much or working too little or...

As this comes up, breathe.

You cannot make everyone happy. Ever. And it is not your job.

So the important thing is to watch this taking place like television. Look at That, happening over There... and know that it is a reflection of the person doing the judging —not of you or how you are handling your life, your grief, your experiences.

There is no one right path.

There is no wrong path either.

There is just the path. This path.

Time

Time passes, and it is marked by a million incremental anniversaries.

The phase of the moon...
day of the month.
month of the year,
season.

Then there are other days—holidays that feel broken and aimless and surreal.

Wedding anniversaries that almost cannot be contemplated. That do not seem possible. Who were those people?

And then there are birthdays.

Our bodies hold memory perhaps better than our minds do.

You may have days where you wake raw and tender and cringing against the upwelling, not knowing that it has all been triggered by the way light slants in through the window.

New Years

At some point it will be New Year's Eve

Celebrations like these can be particularly tough.

But here is something to consider:
This new year? This new year is a year in which *this did not happen*.

Making Peace with Grief

You will develop a strangely familiar relationship with grief.

You are now familiar with how grief comes, sometimes suddenly in a flood of feeling, sometimes seeping in...

You are familiar with the ache of it, the emptiness, the way tears come or the way they don't...

You're familiar with how it grips you, and how it knocks you down, how it settles in heavily, how it steals your breath.

You're familiar with how it somehow always feels brand new.

And now, as time has passed, you're familiar with how it passes too. It comes. It goes. It lurks. It floods in. It ebbs away.

Hello, you say, I know you. And you do.

You do not get extra points for getting over it.
You do not get extra points for holding on to it.

You get extra points for being true to yourself in the moment. The moment may be one of acute grief. It may be a moment of ache and remembering. It may be a moment of joy. It may be a moment of hope.

Honoring where you are in this moment, and this one, and this one and this one and this one... that is the very most important thing.

People Go

Friends may go.

This is one of the hardest parts — losing other people this way.

Suicide has such a societal stigma. It is unthinkable, unimaginable.

Some folks literally may vanish from your life as your experience of loss exposes a vulnerability they may not have ever considered for themselves.

Other folks cannot handle the immensity this kind of loss, this level of grief in those they love or care for. It is too acute. It is just too much.

Other people may be drawn to you now, drawn to your rawness, your hurt, your vulnerability.

Imagine yourself protected by a bubble of light with only you inside. Strengthen those boundaries. Be mindful that not all connections will be good for you. Be aware of how new people make you feel. Say no as often as you need to. This is a good time to practice nearly compulsive self protection.

New News, Old News

You will be at the grocery store. Or out at the park. Or hiking. Or at a museum 100 miles from anywhere you've ever been before. You will run into someone you know. Someone who does not know. Someone who will ask you, innocently, how you are. Or how your beloved is. And you will feel like you are falling backwards into a sudden hell of instant misery.

It may help to imagine what you might say before this happens.

"It has been a really tough year", you might say,"I'm so sorry to have to tell you this, but __ killed themselves in August...I have support, but it is just too hard to talk about as you can imagine. "

These moments are so challenging, because as you deliver the news, it is new news to them. They react with the shock and grief and horror that the new news deserves. You may find yourself trying to comfort them from your own place of acute discomfort. You may find yourself feeling horrible for their grief, for somehow causing it.

And they may ask you the questions you cannot believe people ask. How, when, did you find them...why...

Each time something like this happens, you may feel as if you are being tested.

Sometimes it will happen just when you feel you have your feet under you. You may be feeling a little more like a you that you recognize. A little more stable. A little more happy. A little more whole.

And then facing someone's new, raw grief may take you right back to what feels like the beginning, face to face with your own raw grief.

Be gentle with yourself. Remember grief comes and miraculously goes. Remember that this experience is decidedly non-linear. Remember all you know to be true. Hold yourself gently.

"I'm sorry, but this is just too painful for me to talk about". Remember how to create safe space for yourself, how to exit the conversation, how to turn and walk away.

A Year

And then, somehow, impossibly, it will be a year since they died.

You do not need a calendar to tell you.
You feel it in your bones.

You know it by the feel of the air, the smells and sounds of the season.

You know it in the center of your heart, in the back of your mind, in the middle of your throat.

You know it in the clenched hands, in the dreams that stir up memories and longing, and you walk by and touch a blanket you know they touched, and you may imagine the last few hours of their life even if you do not want to.

You may be flooded with this, even if you think you won't be. It is not a curse of the damned, just the tide coming in. It will come in, flood the lowlands, sweep away all safe places to step and leave slippery mud that holds footprints.

You may not even realize it, but you may find yourself retreating, or picking fights, or walking into doorways.

You may have trouble tying your shoes, or when you bend over to pick up a pencil, your eyes will fill with tears.

There is no right way through this, there is only through.

You may not be angry. Or maybe now, after all this time, you suddenly find yourself furious.

You may not be able to make it through a day without crying. Or you may no longer be that kind of sad.

Whatever you are and wherever you are, you are.

The first year may feel like it has lasted forever, and you may have wondered if you would be able to get through it. You did. You have. You will.

Shame

Shame.

It is so hard to figure out how to soften around shame. Shame has such tenacity, and such a deep reach into the core of our Selves, doesn't it?

Shame holds feelings of complicity or causality. Responsibility.

You didn't do it. You didn't cause it. You didn't create it. You did not choose it.

If someone truly wants to die, they will do everything in their power to make that happen.

Other cultures look at suicide differently, as an indication that the soul's work, for this lifetime, is complete.

If we can imagine that this person's pain was no less

deep than someone with a life-ending illness who chooses to end their life on their terms, how might this change how we view our beloved's choice?

How might it change our grief experience?

Can we open up to the possibility that this was an act, ultimately, of sovereignty?

Someday

Then someday you wake up and it is somehow 7 or 8 or 10 years later.

Grief shifts.
Acuity is replaced by ache.

Even now there are a billion unanswered questions of what if and if only, and no matter how many years have passed, those answers just do not come. They just can't.

The intense upwellings of grief become less frequent. But when it comes, it steals sleep, breaks things at random, leaves you in disarray, and you know by now that it will go. And you know by now, even as you sweep up, that it will come again. The waves will come less frequently... over time you will know this to be true, you will know its rhythm.

Guilt may still feel like heavy clay on thick soled boots. It is so easy to get stuck in guilt and shame. So easy to feel it suck you down into nowhere. There is no solution for this but awareness and resolve and movement. As these familiar feelings come up again and again, choose to raise your eyes up. Look ahead. Step forward under your own power.

10 years is a long time. And it isn't any time at all.

Deep grief may be far from over. Time exposes new layers, and new layers may need new work, new support, new processing, new release... but sometimes there is growth in this work of grieving too. It does not stay the same. It moves, it shifts, it releases, it deepens how we connect with the world, with our own hearts, with our hopes, with what we want, long for, choose for ourselves and those we love.

And there is such beauty. The light changes and as the leaves come out, suddenly there is movement where the branches stood bare a week ago. Bumblebees are flying, however improbably, waiting for the lilac buds to open. The songs of peeper frogs will quiet as the summer heats up, and the cicadas will alert us to the coming autumn. Leaves will color and fall, and waterways will ice over, and snow will come and drift, and the world will be quiet. We are here in this miraculous moment. Let's not miss it.

A Prayer for Healing

May we seek and find the support that we need, knowing that the type of support that we need may change over time.

May we be patient with our grief. Let us soften around the sharp edges, knowing that while time heals, grief can feel new as new layers are exposed.

May we take solace in the no longer unfamiliar rhythm of how grief comes and how it goes.

May the very fact of our immense capacity to love bring healing to those places that are still so raw and filled with disbelief, that are still so filled with regret, that are still so heavy with feelings of responsibility and powerlessness.

May we welcome home the fearful and wounded parts of ourselves, held so carefully and perhaps so secretly for such a long time. All of those pieces we have wished were no longer broken, but are. And those that are still filled with shame.

May we allow ourselves to heal as we can, knowing that time and experience will shift our perspectives, bring us new skills and strengths, a different kind of resilience.

May we open our hearts to connect, love, and be loved.

And, above all, may we learn to trust ourselves again.

Afterword

I want to say this about surviving:
We are stronger than we could ever imagine.

A loved one's suicide is in no way simple. It goes against everything we know to be true in ourselves (the absolute ground truth of wanting to do anything possible to ensure our own survival). And it shakes our confidence: What if we're not as strong as we thought?

We are. We're stronger. We are more resilient than we can imagine.

Your job, now, is survival. Understanding may not ever come. Acceptance is intermittent. Yes, this loss is our truth... but it is not the entirety of our lives, our selves, our identities.

Remember every day that the good memories are real. The good parts of your days now are real. The good feelings you have are real. That all of this complex mosaic is now our truth, the challenges, the grief and the richness of living.

Hold yourself gently and with deep compassion. Return to this self-compassion as often as you can.

Ask for help. Ask again.

Allow yourself to live and live fully. Allow yourself to thrive and be whole.

And in those moments when a surge of grief comes roaring in, remember to breathe, blink, blow breath, and know that it will pass. It will come. And it will go.

Resources

National Suicide Prevention Lifeline
1-800-273-8255

American Foundation for Suicide Prevention
http://www.afsp.org/coping-with-suicide-loss

Alliance of Hope for Suicide Survivors
http://www.allianceofhope.org/survivor_experience/

Acknowledgements

Thank you, beyond thank you, to the amazingly talented Wildwords writers: With special love to Ute, Kathy, Sherry, Suzanne, Suzanne, Nancy, Fran, Tammy, Deborah, Tresa, Lana. Without you, I am not sure I would even know who I am. You held me in such safety and love when I could not hold myself. You listened compassionately to a thousand journal entries as I made my way through the treacherous terrain of early grief. Truly, thank you. Thank you for helping me remember who I am.

Thank you to my love, Doug Sutherland, for loving me in spite of all that you know, and all that you couldn't. I cannot imagine a more beautiful person to share my life with than you. I love you so. You make my heart bigger. I am so glad we found each other.

Thank you to my family of origin: To Sally and Mark and Sarah. No matter where you are, know that you're my sacred ground, my clan, my tribe, my healing circle. Thank you for the gene soup and the free ranging childhood, for my connection to nature and beauty, and for my reverence of all living things.

A profound thank you to Lorraine for seeing what I

was not quite ready to see.

Thank you to Connie for trying to keep me safe, and shepherding me through all of those unimaginably difficult days. I wish you had been able to celebrate this book with me.

Thank you to Toby for seeing me as I am now, and reflecting my vitality back to me. You helped me shift into a new, more coherent place of being.

Thank you to Andy for your kindness, support and love. I feel it. I know it. I am so grateful for the gift of your friendship.

Thank you to Patty Griffin, Deb Talan, and Chris Pureka for your music.

And most of all, thank you Tammy McCracken. Thank you, TammyLove, for all of the things that we both know, and all that words cannot express. I am always and forever grateful for you and to you. You are dear to me in ways that span well beyond what we know of space and time. There is comfort in knowing we will be knowing each other always.

About the Author

Kate Johnson is an artist and writer who lives in New Hampshire with her family. Kate's writings draw heavily from her own personal experiences. Driven by insatiable curiosity and deep compassion, much of her work is about seeking, about the journey from where (and who) we've been to who we're becoming. Her art and writings are informed by her boundless fascination with our ability to mend our broken bits into beautiful mosaics, and the complex inner landscapes hewn and polished by both the tectonic and mundane shifts of our lives and loves. She finds poetry in the tangled thickets of the experience of being human, and is deeply nourished by her spiritual connection to the natural world.

www.kate-johnson.com

Made in the USA
San Bernardino, CA
15 October 2015